Cherokee Phoenix *Print Shop*, *New Echota*,

by the early 1700s. By the American Revolution the first white settlers were in eastern Tennessee.

Indians eagerly traded for European goods—pots, blankets, horses, metal tools, guns, and much more—that became vital to their economies and lifeways. As white traders and frontiersmen married native women, a growing mixed-blood population was found in all tribes. European customs, from dress and language to housing and farming methods, blended with traditional practices. Some tribal leaders practiced plantation agriculture and acquired black slaves. A brilliant Cherokee silversmith, Sequoyah (George Guess), developed a tribal syllabary. Using it, the first American Indian newspaper,

the *Cherokee Phoenix*, began publication in 1828. The Cherokee also developed a written constitution.

These changes deepened old divisions within tribes. Some factions resisted contact with whites and bitterly opposed any accommodations. These groups tended to be full-blood tribal members. Mixed-blood groups, which over time became increasingly wealthy, usually favored closer white relations. Tension among the factions tangled tribal politics, occasionally turning violent.

The most bitter outbreak was among the Creek during the War of 1812. The Red Sticks, a tribal faction militantly opposed to accommodation with whites, overran Fort Mims in southern Alabama, killing more than four hundred whites and mixed-blood Creeks. Under Andrew Jackson a retaliatory campaign lashed back, with whites fighting beside Creek, Choctaw, and Cherokee, crushing the Red Sticks at the Battle of Horseshoe Bend. This defeat marked the last significant military resistance among the Creek, Cherokee, Choctaw, and Chickasaw.

THE GROWING CRISIS.

After the War of 1812, the pressure of white expansion increased enormously. Settlers and planters of the young United States craved rich farmland east

markets of England and the northeastern U.S. By the time Alabama and Mississippi gained statehood in 1817 and 1819, respectively, demands were heard to open Indian lands to whites.

For years many whites, including Thomas Jefferson, called for the removal of Indian peoples westward. They argued that in the hilly woodlands and prairies west of Arkansas, American Indians would be free to live without pressure from white neighbors. In time they might be assimilated into the white mainstream. State officials increased the pressure on tribes to surrender their lands to white farmers. By the 1820s a few thousand Choctaw and Cherokee had emigrated to Arkansas, Texas, and what would become Indian Territory.

Except for the Seminole living in Spanish Florida, however, all tribes had treaties that seemingly guaranteed they would keep their homelands east of the Mississippi. When told to move westward, they answered that they had kept their part of those bargains. Many could point to their past support of American interests. Choctaw and some Cherokee had supported colonists during the American Revolution. Choctaw had battled bravely alongside Jackson at the Battle of New Orleans. The tribes allowed and even welcomed white missionaries. Most of all, they argued, their lands were sacred to their meaning as a people. Leaving that country was like leaving themselves.

Still the pressure grew. By the mid-1820s thousands of white settlers encroached onto Indian lands. Complaints brought no relief. In fact, southern states encouraged this intrusion and demanded that more land be surrendered. The federal government, wary of states' rights issues, did nothing to uphold treaty obligations. Resistance among the Indians stiffened. In 1819 the Cherokee council formally announced that no further land cessions would be considered.

Andrew Jackson's election as President in 1828 brought matters to a head. There was no doubt where he stood in this confrontation. He had made his reputation partly as an Indian fighter (often with the aid of American Indian allies) and had campaigned as a passionate supporter of removal. In 1830 Congress gave him what he wanted—the Removal Act. The act authorized him to negotiate surrender of eastern lands in exchange for other lands in Indian Territory. The government would pay for property left behind, assist with the move westward, help the tribes settle, and protect them in their new homes. For all assurances, the implication was clear: The tribes would emigrate—or else.

FIRST REMOVALS: THE CHOCTAW AND THE CHICKASAW.

Ironically, the first removal efforts were directed at the tribe that had allied most often with the United States in the past—the Choctaw. Their leaders were more angrily divided than in most tribes. Jackson's agents isolated cooperative spokesmen, offered them large grants of prime Mississippi land, and secured the Treaty of Dancing Rabbit Creek (1830). The Choctaw gave up all tribal rights to land east of the Mississippi, but anyone who wished could remain behind and live under state law. All who emigrated would be paid for property left behind. The government was to finance removal and provide food and shelter for the first year in their new homes.

What might seem like a reasonable arrangement soon degenerated into chaos. With word of the treaty, whites crowded onto Choctaw land. Tribal members unfamiliar with white laws were duped out of property and possessions. Other land was seized, and farmsteads were looted. Most Choctaw had no interest in leaving their homes for country they had never seen. In the growing nightmare, with no hope of protection, many reluctantly consented.

The first emigration began in late 1831. Missionaries accompanied some parties and, like the other tribes, the Choctaw brought their considerable numbers of black slaves. Part of the emigration followed a route from northern Mississippi through Tennessee to Memphis, and then across Arkansas, passing through Little Rock, on to southern Indian Territory. A second route left central Mississippi, crossed into southern Arkansas, and joined the first trail.

Pitifully underfunded and poorly administered, the journey was an agonizing disaster. By deep winter travelers were on muddy, frozen roads through Arkansas, suffering terribly from temperatures plunging below zero. To avoid the cold, the next year's emigration was scheduled for summer, but those exiles were stricken by fevers and laid low by stifling heat. By a cruel coincidence, the nation's first epidemic of Asiatic cholera struck the Mississippi valley just as the Choctaw were crossing it. Witnesses to this two-year torment were appalled. The famous French visitor to America, Alexis de Toqueville, came upon the Choctaw late in 1831:

It was then the middle of winter, and the cold was unusually severe; the snow had frozen hard upon the ground, and the river was drifting huge masses of ice.... I saw [the Choctaw] embark to pass the mighty river, and never will that solemn spectacle fade from my remembrance. No cry, no sob, was heard among the assembled crowd. All were silent.

The Chickasaw, kinsmen of the Choctaw, began their ordeal in a somewhat better position. Although its terms were never fully honored, the Treaty of Pontotoc (1832) provided a good price for their surrendered lands in northern Mississippi. They were allowed to organize their own emigration. Like other tribes, they saw their land invaded by white squatters, but they were given the chance to choose what they considered the best of Indian Territory—a southern portion along the Texas border.

Even these advantages turned against the Chickasaw. For their trek west in 1837, they followed the Choctaw's northern route. Ample funds were committed to have supplies waiting along the road, but contractors, charging grossly inflated prices, sent far more than was needed. Hundreds of barrels of pork and other food, left in the summer sun, were worthless by the time the emigrants got to them. Far behind schedule, slowed by poor roads, and bilked by merchants along the way, they were caught by winter far from their destination. "I am here starving with the Chickasaws," a government agent wrote. Near the end travelers were hit by smallpox, which they passed on to the neighboring Choctaw. A withering drought in 1838 further devastated the roughly six thousand persons who completed the journey.

Removal of the Choctaw and

Winter added to the torment of removal along the Mississippi River.

Chickasaw set the pattern. Other tribes were pushed from their lands by similar maneuvers. All would suffer on the long roads westward. Details varied, but in the end, all faced the dilemma described by a Choctaw leader, Chief Harkins, who addressed white Mississippians watching his boatload of emigrants about to cast off from their home shore. "Some say we are leaving of our own choice," Harkins said. But not so:

> We found ourselves like a benighted stranger following false guides, until he was surrounded on every side by fire and water. A distant view on the opposite shore encouraged the hope; to remain would be inevitable annihilation. Who would hesitate, or who would say that his plunging into the water was his own voluntary act?

REMOVAL BY FORCE: THE CREEK. More whites crowded into Alabama than any other part of the coastal South after the War of 1812. When thousands of people invaded Creek lands, unhindered by state officials, the federal government's response, once again, was to argue that emigration was the only practical solution. Creek leaders steadfastly refused.

In 1832 Creek negotiators accepted what seemed a generous concession. The Treaty of Washington surrendered the vast tribal claim of five million acres in eastern Alabama, but two million acres were set aside as allotments for those wishing to stay. No one was required to leave. Families could remain as long as they liked, with full title as owners. If they chose to emigrate, they could sell and move west with the help of the national government. Perhaps most important, the treaty promised to prevent local seizures of land and to protect all civil rights.

Immediately, however, this arrangement fell apart. As soon as Creek lands began to be surveyed, speculators and swindlers used their imaginations to find ways to defraud Indians out of their land titles. They threatened the vulnerable and lied to the illiterate to get their "X" on a bill of sale. They smoothed the way with alcohol, rigged gambling games, foreclosed on credit for goods sold at bloated prices, or simply gave forged documents to cooperative officials. The Creek's situation, precarious before the fraud began, turned rapidly worse. Most sank into despair. An army officer reported that traders, "like locusts...have devoured [the Indians'] substance and inundated their homes with whiskey." The Creek were "brow beat, and cowed... and depressed with the feeling that they have no adequate protection in the United States, and no capacity for self protection in themselves."

Swindles and seizures continued until, by 1836, most Creek land had passed into white hands. Only a few hundred persons had chosen to emigrate. The rest—about fifteen thousand—lived precariously on land the state now said belonged to white newcomers. At this point, a small faction of Lower Creek began attacking nearby settlers and travelers. The assaults soon stopped, and even a leading state newspaper called the outcry that followed a "diabolical scheme" by land grabbers to keep the Indians "from maintaining their just rights." Lewis Cass, secretary of war and a vocal advocate of removal, quickly ordered the army to move in, crush resistance, and round up all Creek and take them westward.

Troops met virtually no resistance in arresting about sixteen hundred people accused of taking part or sympathizing in the "Creek War." Men were shackled, handcuffed, and taken by steamboat from Mobile, Alabama, to the Mississippi and upriver to Arkansas. By midsummer, with women and children following close behind, the prisoners were marched to Indian Territory by a route roughly following the Arkansas River. Inadequate supplies, wretched food, decrepit equipment, and intense heat made for conditions that shocked many

observers. One had "never seen so wretched and poor a body of Indians....They really have nothing."

The huge majority of Creek had no part in the short rebellion and, in fact, several hundred volunteered to suppress it. Nonetheless, soldiers rounded up nearly all tribal members and ordered them into groups of two thousand or three thousand. Starting in midsummer and continuing deep into winter, they were taken west under military escort. With large numbers of slaves, they followed several routes from eastern Alabama through northern Mississippi and far-southwestern Tennessee. Beyond the Mississippi they moved across Arkansas by much the same path taken by earlier prisoners.

With supplies and preparations appallingly poor, the route through Arkansas became a gauntlet to run as foraging and thefts by hungry emigrants brought reprisals from bands of angry locals. The ill and exhausted lagged behind until the various groups bled into a continuous stream of suffering. By winter, conditions were desperate:

Thousands...are entirely destitute of shoes or cover of any kind for their feet; many are almost naked, and but few of them [have] anything more than a light dress....In this destitute condition they are wading in cold mud, or are hurried on over the frozen ground.... Many of them...die, and are thrown by the side of the road, and are covered over only with brush, etc.—where they remain until devoured by the wolves.

The last groups reached their destination by early spring.

The Creek were the only large southeastern tribe never to sign a treaty of removal. They were removed nonetheless, through armed force. Their estimated losses were the highest of all the removed tribes. As many as one out of four died before the ordeal of the Creek Trail of Tears was over.

ORDEAL: THE CHEROKEE. As the easternmost tribe, the Cherokee for years felt pressure to open their lands to outsiders. With Jackson's election, tribal leaders knew demands would intensify. Then came news in July 1829 that gold had been discovered in creeks around Dahlonega, Georgia. Hundreds of gold seekers flooded the area, seizing promising sites and building ramshackle camps in what was to become the richest gold strike east of the Mississippi. Georgian officials acted quickly to wrestle this land away from its native people.

Their strategy was simple. They would make it impossible for the Cherokee to live as they wished. In 1829 the Georgia legislature declared Cherokee land confiscated and promised to hand it over to whites. No Cherokee

would be allowed to mine gold. The Cherokee tribal government was abolished and its laws declared void. Any Cherokee who discouraged another from emigrating westward would be imprisoned. Cherokees could not testify against whites in court, and they were forbidden to hold any kind of meeting, even for religious services, unless they were assembling to surrender their land.

The tribal council responded with a law of its own, putting in writing the dictate that any Cherokee who disposed of a single acre without council consent would be put to death. Facing the tribe's dilemma, an elderly chief, Womankiller, spoke for many others. He said that his people were bound to whites by "the golden chain of friendship." Now many said that national and state governments were determined to "act the tyrant" and kill the Cherokee for their land. Even death was better than abandoning their home:

> My sun of existence is now fast approaching to its setting, and my aged bones will soon be laid underground, and I wish them laid in the bosom of this earth we have received from our fathers who had it from the Great Being above. When I shall sleep in forgetfulness, I hope my bones will not be deserted by you.

The council appealed to the courts of the nation that now threatened them. The Cherokee argued that a state had no right to interfere with national government treaties guaranteeing Indian peoples land and independence. Washington, the Cherokee said, must step in and protect them from Georgia's assault. In two crucial decisions (*Cherokee Nation v. Georgia*, 1831 *and Worcester v. Georgia*, 1832) the U.S. Supreme Court agreed that Georgia's laws against the Cherokee were "repugnant" to the Constitution.

President Jackson refused to protect the Cherokee from Georgia's laws. Instead he took advantage of a bitter division among tribal leaders and sent agents to negotiate with the "treaty party," whose leaders included Elias Boudinot, former editor of the *Cherokee Phoenix*. Although the group had opposed removal for years, they now argued that the Cherokee had no other practical option.

Other leaders and the great majority of Cherokee still opposed removal. The Cherokee identified intimately with the forested hills and green valleys that had been their home for scores of generations. Principal Chief John Ross argued that his people had every right to stay and be protected. He knew moving thousands of families hundreds of miles would be a tremendous ordeal.

Jackson's negotiators drew up a removal treaty. In October 1835 the Cherokee council at Red Clay rejected it. Even Ridge and Boudinot joined the majority against it. Jackson then tried another strategy, announcing that his agents would negotiate another treaty at the Cherokee capital of New Echota in December 1835. Those Cherokee who failed to appear would be counted in favor of any treaty made. Only three hundred to five hundred

attended. At the conclusion of negotiations, not more than one hundred persons—out of a population of approximately seventeen thousand—voted on the treaty.

Under its terms, the Cherokee surrendered all land east of the Mississippi River. The government was to pay $5 million (although it never did) and provide land for resettlement in Indian Territory near the Osage people along the Arkansas and Grand Rivers. The federal government agreed to finance the exodus. Emigrants were promised support during their first year building new homes (although this pledge would be largely ignored). The entire operation had to be completed within two years of treaty ratification.

Ross and other leaders reacted

with outrage, as did prominent whites. Nonetheless, after heated debate the Senate approved the treaty by a single vote in May 1836. Jackson announced that no further challenges would be heard. In fact, he said, the Cherokee government would not exist until reorganized west of the Mississippi. All tribal members who failed to leave by April 1837 would violate the law of the land.

CHEROKEE EXODUS. As the deadline approached, only about two thousand Cherokee people had emigrated. The rest, about sixteen thousand people with about sixteen hundred slaves and some free blacks, remained on their land while Ross pled their case. He traveled to Washington, D.C., carrying petitions with 15,665 names repudiating the treaty, but the Senate would not receive it. Meanwhile, white Georgians pressed closer against Cherokee lands, eyeing cabins and plantations. General John Wool, sent to guard against Indian insurrection, found instead "the whole scene...has been nothing but a heart-rending one," with peaceful Cherokee families threatened by whites who were "like vultures, ready to pounce upon their prey and strip them of everything they have."

In late spring of 1838 Major General Winfield Scott arrived with five regiments. Helped by four thousand militia and volunteers, he was to seize all Cherokee and confine them in stockades until they could be taken to Indian Territory. The roundup began on May 26, 1838. Squads swept through the hills. Families took only what they could carry—clothes, valuables, a few precious mementos. Everything else— the fruits of generations of labor— was left behind.

Scott sternly ordered "every possible kindness" be shown to the deportees. Soldiers generally complied, but others, drawn mostly from locals who had spent years waiting the chance, turned immediately to looting. Cherokee memories were often horrific:

Families at dinner were startled by the sudden gleam of bayonets in the doorway and rose up to be driven with blows and oaths along the weary miles of trail that led to the stockade. Men were seized in their fields or going along the road, women were taken from their [spinning] wheels and children from their play. In many cases, in turning for one last look as they crossed the ridge, they saw their homes in flames, fired by the lawless rabble that followed on the heels of the soldiers to loot and pillage.

Years later one of the volunteers looked back: "I fought through the civil war and saw men shot to pieces and slaughtered by the thousands, but the Cherokee removal was the cruelest work I ever knew."

The uprooted, including hundreds of slaves, were taken first to thirty-one temporary camps near Cherokee towns. Later they were moved to eleven internment centers, one in Alabama and the rest in Tennessee, to await removal. Conditions in these places became nightmarish. Crowded together in filthy conditions, plagued by alternating heat and rain, the Cherokee suffered from whooping cough, measles, pleurisy, fever, and other maladies. Dysentery was rampant. By late June deaths were mounting, with children and elderly most at risk. Many army officers tried to lessen the suffering—to no avail. The dying continued throughout the summer. Survivors were weak and demoralized.

Removal spread out over nearly a year. The first families began their trip in early June 1838. The last straggled into Indian Territory in mid-March 1839.

The thousands of exiles moved along several routes by different means. Some fared better than others. All would look back on the passage as their people's greatest ordeal.

For about twenty-eight hundred people, the way west was by water. At Ross's Landing (now Chattanooga), they boarded flatboats, following the winding course of the Tennessee River through northern Alabama, Tennessee, and Kentucky to the Ohio River. They traveled by steamboat down the Ohio and Mississippi Rivers, then up the Arkansas River toward the hillier country of eastern Indian Territory. Their circuitous route covered more than 1,200 miles. During one of the hottest and driest summers of the century, the Arkansas River dropped so low that hundreds covered the last stage by foot and wagon. The sick and elderly suffered terribly in suffocating heat and choking dust along rocky, primitive roads. Every day there were new graves to dig. Seventy died from dysentery along Lee's Creek, close to the journey's end, when famished marchers gorged on green corn and peaches.

Once Ross saw his only option was removal under armed guard, he contracted with the government to oversee the rest of the exodus. The remaining captive Cherokee were organized into thirteen groups. In the holding camps, their livestock and belongings were seized by whites as payment for debts, often bogus. Property was "robbed of us in open daylight," a leader wrote

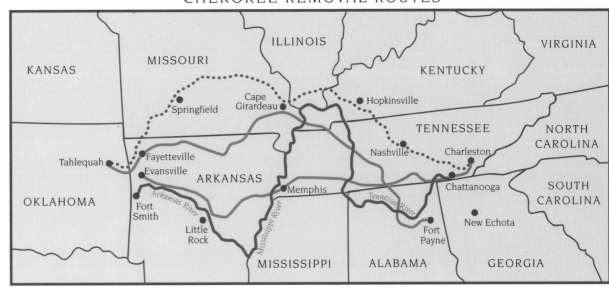

Trail of Tears National Historic Trail: ●●●●Land Route ▬▬Water Route ▬▬▬Other Major Routes

Ross, by thieves who "know we are in a defenseless situation." The first party left at the start of October, the last in early December.

Overland removal followed three main routes. The oldest, youngest, and sickest rode in the wagons, crowded among supplies and possessions. Confinement in camps left many weak and ill. Some travelers, notably those in the treaty party, received more support than others, but the general government allocation of sixteen cents a day per person fell far short of even basic needs. By postponing departure, Ross avoided the awful heat and fevers of summer, but by cruel luck, winter 1838-39 began with torrential rains, leaving emigrants slogging through deep mud.

The weather then turned viciously cold. A wealthy few traveled in carriages. But, as one observer wrote,

> [The] multitudes go on foot—even aged females, apparently nearly ready to drop into the grave, were traveling with heavy burdens attached to the back—on the sometimes frozen ground...with no covering for the feet except what nature had given them.... Some carry a downcast dejected look...others a wild frantic appearance as if about to burst the chains of nature and pounce like a tiger upon their enemies.

Perhaps the worst time was at Green's Ferry on the Mississippi, where exhausted crowds waited, often for weeks, to cross the

Cherokee land left behind, Oconaluftee Creek, Great Smokey Mountains National Park

ice-choked river into Missouri. Scholar James Mooney spoke with survivors much later:

> The lapse of over half a century |has| not sufficed to wipe out the memory of the miseries of that halt beside the frozen river, with hundreds of sick and dying penned up in wagons or stretched upon the ground, with only a blanket overhead to keep out the January blast.

Malnourished by a diet of cornmeal, beans, and a little salt pork, travelers suffered from dysentery, pellagra, pneumonia, and a range of other diseases. Government doctors, one per every thousand travelers, did their best, but they could barely keep up. At virtually every camp Cherokee were left behind in poorly marked graves as family and friends continued the march. A survivor later recalled:

> Long time we travel on way to new land....Women cry and made sad wails. Children cry and many men cry, and all look sad like when friends die, but they say nothing and just put heads down and keep on go towards West. Many days pass and people die very much.

By the end of March 1839 the last of the twelve thousand Cherokee straggled in. John Ross traveled most of the way by boat. Along the way he buried his wife, Quatie. She was far from alone.

Missionary doctor Elizno Butler estimated that more than four thousand Cherokee died—nearly a fifth of the Cherokee population.

WAR AND REMOVAL: THE SEMINOLE.

The fiercest physical resistance came from the Seminole. Living in the panhandle of Spanish Florida, they faced less interference from whites, and so were reluctant to surrender their relative freedom. They refused the government's demand to surrender slaves and free blacks—part of their society. The government required the Seminole to merge with the Creek if they emigrated west. Although many were descended from Creek, the Seminole demanded recognition as a separate and distinct people.

Relations with whites had been contentious after Spain transferred Florida to the United States in 1821. The Seminole felt increasing pressure to open their lands to white farmers and planters. Tensions escalated into late 1835. Seminoles killed their government agent and virtually annihilated an army command sent to force their removal. They would resist "till the last drop of the Seminole's blood has moistened the dust of his hunting ground," one of their leaders wrote.

Thus began one of the longest wars in American history. For seven years army troops and Indians recruited from the Creek, Shawnee, Delaware, and others, pressed into Florida's thick woodlands and steamy swamps, destroying camps and stores of food, keeping the fugitives on the run. The cost was enormous. Troops sickened and died from malaria and other diseases. The Seminole fought back with remarkable tenacity and inflicted terrible losses. Their most effective leader was Oceola, the warrior who had sworn to fight to "the last drop of blood." He and other leaders—Wildcat, Billy Bowlegs, Crazy Alligator, Jumper, and Abraham, a black who had risen high in tribal affairs—rallied opposition that left army commander Gen. Thomas S. Jesup frustrated and humiliated.

The government's overwhelming force took its toll on the Seminole. Families were reduced to starvation, and grinding warfare wore at their resolve. Soldiers captured small groups of fugitives, often in twos and threes. Others surrendered. In a widely condemned act, Jesup ordered Oceola taken during a meeting under a flag of truce. Oceola died early in 1839, imprisoned in Charleston, South Carolina. Still, led by Wildcat and Billy Bowlegs, some continued to fight and elude capture as they withdrew deep into the swamplands. About fifteen hundred white troops died— one for every two Seminoles captured and deported.

In 1842 the government decided that further pursuit was not worth the effort. Seminole who were not apprehended were allowed to remain in the Everglades. Some of their descendants live there today.

Captured Seminole were taken westward on their own Trail of Tears. Of 407 in a group removed in 1836, twenty-five died by the time they arrived by steamboat at Fort Smith. The next three weeks were far worse. Pounded by rain, plodding through sloughs of mud, they crept toward their new homes in Texas, on many days burying three or four persons beside a sodden camp. During the two-month journey, eighty-seven Seminole died—about one of every five. Between 1838 and 1842, those who had been captured or had surrendered were taken to lands along the Illinois River in Indian Territory. Scores of Seminole blacks were returned to slavery among whites and Creek Indians who had fought with the army. Deported Seminole left behind their possessions, their homeland, and their independence. In January 1843, as the last group was being taken to a ship that would carry them away, one of their leaders made a last request to the officer in charge:

The Indians wished to give the war yell. I gave permission & it was done, but soon afterwards a revulsion of feeling seemed to overcome the whole of them; for on nearing the wharf the Indians

Property valuations from first Board of Cherokee Commissioners

No 185   Au'se'ke'Ta

+   Improvements
              Two Run Creek

Dwelling House 18ft sqr. hewed, neat &c $200 00
Do. 18 by 16 split logs, 1 floor, c. roof & chimney   100 00
Stable 16ft sqr. 20 logs   very neat   40 00
Set of Cribs under one Roof   25 00
1 Do 18 by 14 00. logs   20 00
23 Peach Trees @ 1.50   34 50
3 Apple   do @ 3.ea   9 00
Yard Lot 2 acrs   10 00
87 Acres unp'd Land   @ 8   136 00
                                          $ 574 50

No 186   Peggy Moore

+   Improvements
              Two Run Creek

Dwelling House 18ft sqr. 10. logs, 1 floor, c. roof & cly $ 150 00
Kitchen 16ft sqr.   "   "   "   "   40 00
Crib 12 by 8ft split logs   15 00
Ditto 16. 00. 10. ro logs.   good   20 00
Fodder House 15ft sqr 10. logs   20 00
30 Peach Trees @ 1.50   45 00
40 Acres imp'd Land @ 8   320 00
27.   "   "   " on Etowah @ 10   270 00
                                          $ 880 00

Rent on 15 Do 2 yr @ 3.50 $ 105 —

appeared to be struck with the conviction that they were now, indeed, in our power.

WE ARE STILL HERE. The great majority of Indian peoples east of the Mississippi suffered removal to the west. Each had its own story of dispossession and deprivation. Dozens of tribes—from as far away as New York and the upper Great Lakes—were crowded into Indian Territory. Removal, however, was never completed. In the Southeast, besides the Seminole remaining in the Everglades, about four hundred Cherokees in the North Carolina mountains eluded capture. This group—called the Oconaluftee Cherokee or the Eastern Band of Cherokee—trace their origin to an 1819 treaty that gave them American citizenship and an allotment of land not belonging to the Cherokee Nation. In 1866 they were granted state citizenship. About ten thousand now live on a reservation in western North Carolina.

The Poarch Creek band of Creek stayed in southern Alabama, near Atmore. Thousands of Choctaw are a vital part of Mississippi society. Many Creek and Cherokee managed to break away during the journey and settle along the way in Missouri and Arkansas.

For those who walked the trail,